Thule

Poems
by Benn Sowerby

Order this book online at www.trafford.com
or email orders@trafford.com

Most Trafford titles are also available at major online book retailers.

Note for Librarians: A cataloguing record for this book is available from Library
and Archives Canada at www.collectionscanada.ca/amicus/index-e.html

Printed in Victoria, BC, Canada.

ISBN: 978-1-4269-1136-1

*Our mission is to efficiently provide the world's finest, most comprehensive
book publishing service, enabling every author to experience success.
To find out how to publish your book, your way, and have it available
worldwide, visit us online at www.trafford.com*

Trafford rev. 08/24/09

Trafford
PUBLISHING www.trafford.com

North America & international
toll-free: 1 888 232 4444 (USA & Canada)
phone: 250 383 6864 ♦ fax: 812 355 4082

by the same author

Contents

To One that Beckons

I have not sought thee.-
Thou hast found me out.
Yet, 'though on a restless sea
I drift in doubt,
Yet I will follow thee.
Dim paths I know,
Unfaltering, thou leadest me;
But down them blow,
Surely, fresh winds, and 'though
Even sorrows, strange,
Illimitable with me go,
I seek but change.

Cheated

I did not know—
My youth was all to me,
I could not know
That such a time would be.

Beauty in soft, low tones
Lured me, and blinded my sight.
Now cold the wind that moans
Around me in the night.

Cheated of all, alone,
Deluded I sit and see
Youth, beauty, joy, all gone;
And none to comfort me.

Song

How tenderly love's lilies greet the dawn,
Opening their cups to drink the morning dew,
And filling with sweet perfume all the air.
    Yet with more beauty do you meet the morn,
    And more than lilies all will I love you,
    And on your soft, white shoulder banish care.

At evening, when the lilies close their cups,
Bemused, and drunk with ecstacy night-roused,
I'll seek the dreamy whiteness of your form.
    And, as of evening dews the lily sups,
    Then closes, from your lips I'll drink till drowsed,
    Then fold your form to mine, still, pale, and warm

Lines

Why will you ever steal into my thoughts
When I would think of other, happier things ?

Of fabulous dream-palaces and courts,
Of jasper and onyx where the bulbul sings,
Where crystal fountains spill their dazzling lights
On emerald lawns beneath pale turquoise skies,
Where flash gay birds bright-plumed in wheeling flights,
And deep in leaf-green quiet glittering eyes,
Burn with a still intensity from shade.
And there when evening breezes, cool and fresh,
Whisper faint music down each grassy glade
Dance dark-eyed maidens, scarlet-lipped, whose flesh
Shines in pale moonlight silver and ivory,
Now lost in shade, now gleaming out again.

Till you creep in to shatter the harmony,
And sadden me once more with unfelt pain.

"Find out moonshine. . . ."

Softly in the evening
Whispered a small, faint breeze
In the glimmering light of the cold, pale moon
Through the trees,

"Who seeks the border of dreamland
"Vainly this still night,
"Follow thy fancy's fluting in the
"Clear moonlight."

And I rose and followed lightly
Through shadows dark and deep.
And wandered away to distant dreamland
Through the fields of sleep.

Then far in a wood in the darkness
I came on a small, clear pool,
Where an old oak straddled a boulder
Like a stool.

And up through the water sliding
Shone a shoulder slim and bare,
And there floated a nymph before me
With moon-beam-spangled hair.

One moment, ere slipping downward,
The curves of her body gleam,
As with scarlet lips scarce-parted
She whispers, "Vain is dream."

Sadly I wandered onward,
And the night air falling chill
Quickened my step, that I passed un-noting
Valley and hill.

And I came to the end of my journey
On a moonlit, sandy shore,
With but the sound of the lapping ripples,
No more.

Till, black on the far horizon,
Rearing its neck like a tree,
Trailing lank sea-weeds, a creature comes swiftly,
Cleaving the sea,

Snorting through quivering nostrils,
Noble and fierce and strange,
Scanning his path with gleaming eyes
That slowly range.

Then, swerving round so swiftly
That his body is lost in spray,
He leaves me in fearful wonder.
And rides away . . . . .

Strange was that land and its creatures
I knew, but I must not stay;
One must not dwell on its wonders;
Madness lies that way.

So I turned my back in the moonlight
On the lonely shore and the sea

And hastened back to this other world
Of reality.

Ah! would I might leave for ever
This world and this curious me,
And wander away with my dreams and fancies,
Free.

Thule

Bare to the dim horizon stretched the land,
    Where halted, with haggard eyes
Straining in vain, that small and wearied band
    Beneath blue, endless skies.

Scentless, the still, calm air wreathed overhead.
    No creature was there save those.
Silence unbroken buried all hope, all dread,
    While, speechless, they huddled close.

Till the voice of one shrilled on the fainting air,
    "Is but this our journey's end?
"So far have we voyaged—for this alone our care?"
    Silence still echoes send.

Echo

Will it never come again,
The torture and the bliss?
There was pleasure in the pain
Of one long-remembered kiss.
Will it never come again?
     Never again!

Is all my joy so soon,
So swiftly, surely past?
Perhaps I might have known
Such wonder could not last.
Yet is it past so soon?
     All past. All past!

And will delight, no more
Wake echo in the glade?
Cursed be the winds that tore
The leaves from that sweet shade!
Is all but sighs, no more?
     No more. No more!

Ghosts

When the shadows leap up higher on the walls,
Fantastic figures sinking into gloom,
As the last flame leaps up and quickly falls,
Darkening the room,

They close in round me silent as I sit,
Eagerly pressing everywhere about,
And, where the last lights dying faintly flit,
Strange eyes gleam out.

I feel their curious fingers on my face—
Is that a murmur that I seem to hear,
Or is it fancy as grotesque thoughts race—
Until in fear

Shivering in the cold, dim blank of night,
I stir the dying embers to a flame,
And with the brightening of the faint, warm light
A sudden rush— and all's once more the same.

Protest

Disclose thy face
To these, dull, straining eyes,
Or else be gone.
For me your mystery is a well of sighs.

Trouble me not
With these half-hidden things.
I would be free
From the vain striving your fair presence brings.

Wind in the Apple Tree

Low sank the sun, and high in the apple tree
The songs of the birds lulled suddenly to cease.
Softly swept the breeze through the blossoms of the
        apple tree,
Bearing the scent of an unimagined peace.

Stilly sank the air as silently I listened there,
I Iearkening for the voice of one I felt but could not see.
Slowly waved the blossoms, and drowsily they glistened
        there,
While darker shone the leaves in the depths of the tree.

Suddenly the apple blossoms stirred and were shaken,
And a spirit seemed to wander, lightly dancing on the
        breeze,
Whispering in the twilight, care-free, forsaken.
"Who would be tied in such narrow bounds as these?

" Liberty is happiness, and joy to know the meaning of
"The sounds and the scents that float upon the air,
"Mingling in a harmony, whose music drowns the
        keening of
"The sadness of memories that lie beyond despair."

Re-birth

These men that pass me in the street
With busy noise of shuffling feet

Have never felt the joy in things
That I have felt, a joy that sings

In every murmur of the wind,
Like Eden's breeze ere Adam sinned.

They have not known the living glow
That I have known. "How should they know?"

"How should they know?" my thoughts complain,
"For they have never felt your pain."

Would I could help them, deaf and blind,
To find the happiness I find

In life. Instead, they are content,
On dull, prosaic nothings bent.

Would they but listen, I could yet
Shew them strange pleasures here, and let

Them feel my joy in earthly things . . . .
But, hush now! hear that lark that sings,

As he mounts skyward, loud and long.
What rapture in his sparkling song!

A song that lifts to heaven's cope,
And echoes with immortal hope . . . . .

"You cannot help them. Leave them, then,"
My thoughts cry out, "unhappy men,

"Knowing not what they miss. But you!
"Why should you miss all pleasure too?"

And, wondering at their light-less earth,
I mutely turn to my re-birth.

The Vagrant

There are some who say
That the winds lament
In mournful tones when the year is spent.

I have come far to-day
With the wind in my ear
Wailing, it seemed, for the dying year,

As I took my way
Among naked trees,
Oppressed by the sadness of strange decrees.

But the gorse burned gay
On the open moor
When I left the wood's brown-leaf-piled floor.

And come what may,
I've a heart that burns
With the joy that only a vagrant earns.

Firelight

The shadows thickened curiously there
Upon the wall, and in the darkened air
I saw, turning from the warm, wavering light,
Two fiery eyes that shimmered through the night.
I heard frail, gauzy wings that beat in vain,
Fluttering strangely on the window-pane.
Then dim, vast silence drooped again forlornly.
"A friend? An enemy?"
The sinking embers rustle in the grate.
The clock ticks on (who cares?), "Too late.
                    Too late."

The Flame

From the shadows deep, unstirring,
Clothing silence in the night,
A moth flits, softly whirring,
In swift, impassioned flight.

Some strange dream-wonder lures her
On the keen, still air,
And the candle's light assures her
As with mazed and steady stare.

She wings to its effusion
In the night's chill breath,
But to know her dream delusion
In the ecstacy of death.

Youth's Beauty

Haunt me not still
With vain imaginings.
Thy memory can but kill
That ease oblivion brings.

I love thee not:
Nor have I clung to thee:
Almost I had forgot
What once thou wert to me.

I would be free.
Yet ever must I bow
To thee, false fair? Leave me!
Ah! leave me now!

A Fancy

The moon seemed very far away to-night,
    Enwreathed in haze of mist,
As pale but steady shone her light
    Where she kept lonely tryst.

And still, pale, distant as she hung,
    She showed earth very small,
An unconsidered toy among
    Stars hid in the mist's pall.

The Old Mill

High on the rain-swept,
    Windy hill,
Gaunt and grey, stands the
    Ancient mill.
Though the wind sweeps round each
    Broken vane,
Long years now it has
    Ground no grain.
But, gazing over the
    Land it sees,
Creaking loud at each
    Feeble breeze,
The ways of that curious
    Creature—man.
And round it turns, each
    Side to scan.
Then, waving its naked
    Arms in air,
It shifts again, and
    Groans despair.

"Shut the Lattice, Mary"

Shut the lattice, Mary.
　　The night air's cold.
I cannot sleep so easily
　　Now I am old.

But the air to-night has gathered
　　Fresh scents from all about.
And would you close the lattice
　　To shut it's freshness out?

Draw the curtain, Mary.
　　The moon's too bright.
I cannot sleep as easily
　　As that to-night

But the moon to-night's so lovely
　　With its pale, still ray.
And would you draw the curtain
　　To hide its light away?

Shut the lattice, Mary.
　　The moon's too bright.
I cannot sleep as easily
　　As once to-night.

Experience

Many things there be
Whose worth we do not prize
When given free
But whose loss is sighs.

I have lost much
And ever I seek in vain
A loveliness such
As comes not again.

The Wanderer

In dreams I saw a wanderer
    Threading his lonely way
Over a country faint in mist,
    With no sun's ray.

The path he followed, stooping,
    He knew was a way well worn,
As vaguely he searched with troubled eyes,
    In vain, forlorn.

And a bird in the distance uttered
    A mocking and eerie sound,
Hidden from the eyes of the traveller,
    Whom the mist closed round.

Then he raised his voice on the night-wind,
    And called in a loud, clear tone,
But only the distant echoes answered
    With a far, faint moan.

Footsore and faint was the wanderer,
    Desolate and lone,
As despairing he turned to the track once more,
    Groped in the mist, and was gone.

Cock-crow

Why does the cock crow up the dawn,
    When such a dawn as this?
The murky air broods thick, forlorn ;
    Still every voice but his.

Even the happy lark forgets
    To mount his song of mirth.
Why greet a heavy day that sets
    Its weight on all the earth?

The Hermit

I shunned the noise of busy feet,
The murmuring voices of the crowd;
The hubbub of the city street
Hung heavy o'er me like a cloud.

I left the purl of streams in woods
That echo with the song of birds,
For the reality that broods
Remote from music and from words.

I seek in solitude to find,
Beyond the reflexes of thought
In the dim archives of the mind,
A truth none yet has ever taught.

A Memory

There was a garden. I can see it clearly.
The mossy paths flanked by tall hollyhocks,
The mingled scents of rose and thyme and box
Freshening the air, and apple blossom too.
But now again the memory eludes me,
So that I see one corner only which mocks
My thoughts of that fair garden that I knew,
A dusty corner where tall nettles grew.

The Lure

The moonlight slanted idly down,
Silent and pallid, strangely cool;
A curving willow leaned to drown
Its drooping locks in the shining pool.

Deep in long grass the nightshade stood
And spread its fruit of glittering jet,
Like some delicious fairy food
Upon a moon-lit platter set.

And voices whispered through the sedge,
With luring, listless tone,
Of lands that lie beyond the edge
Of the furthest we have known.

Grief

Pause, pause.
Unthinking sorrow will not ease
So deep a grief.
Can tears blot out such memories as these!
Nay, seek elsewhere relief.
Weep not, for by each vain-shed tear
Such sorrow is but deepened. The true cure
Lies far, alas! from here.

Aspiration

Look not, wild heart, toward those distant hills
In beauty burning, though the spirit wills.
On each dim crest mysterious shadows move;
Yet seek them not lest they but mirage prove.
Look back once more! All beauty is not spent.
Can'st thou not be, as of old thou wast, content?
Gloom-stilled the day! Uncertain that far quest!
Thou'rt weary: calm thyself, wild heart, and rest.

Evening

Twilight falls swiftly on the hill,
And yet more swiftly in the valley until
With star-lit darkness night broods chill
   Above the slumbering earth.

Dark figures loom where creepers clung;
Black fruit where rosy berries hung;
And silence where the linnet sung
   So sweetly not long since.

Soft gleam the distant fields of sleep,
Where deep in dew pale moon-flowers peep,
And high above the misty steep
   Dream communes with the stars.

To-night

Last night I sought the nightingale
That carolled in the dell,
For her sadness fraught with happiness
Told the joy I could not tell.

But to-night I'll seek the ghostly owl
Among the dark pine tops,
And the glooming shadows' solitude
In the moon-lit, silent copse.

At Dawn

A late star hangs in the cold, grey sky
Above the silent roofs;
Three men ride out, and the white flakes fly
From their horses' muffled hoofs.

The dawn breaks clear above the hill
On pastures deep in snow,
And through the morning silence shrill,
One hears a farm cock crow.

And one unnoticed turns aside
With swiftly-curious stare
To see, where the crystal snow seemed dyed,
Only a robin there.

But one, who watches the distant skies
For Dawn's unclouded birth,
An early-winging lark descries,
Ascending from the earth.

Autumn

The sun shone. Gay
On a leafless spray,
A bird, shrill-voiced,
Rejoiced
In the autumn day
With song untaught.
Such beauty caught
In the memory
Will be
Always dear to me,
A moment of loveliness,
Transcending thought.

The Prisoner

Sigh not forlornly! I am near,
Companion in thy dear distress.
Peace, peace! Does not yet the moon shine clear?
And gleams not yet each silken tress

Of the honeyed jasmine rambling there
On the rain-worn, crumbling stone!
Such delicate beauty is all too rare:
Yet fairer far will be thy own,

When thou shalt journey into light,
Freed from these rusty prison bars,
As slants a far meteor through the night,
Amid the galaxy of stars.

Regret

How often here, between these walls of space,
    Beneath this all-perplexing roof of Time,
The lovely vision of a youthful face
    Has cleared and brightened hopeless eyes long-
    dimmed.
Vainly aspiring thoughts in fancy climb
    To peer beyond the hills of No Return,
Till, thus recalled by loveliness clear-limned,
    They seek no longer truths none here may learn.

In this tall mansion, where I sadly sit
    To warm myself before the fading fire,
My last dim taper is already lit:
    Yet endless seem the hours. 0, would that thou,
Of whose loved image I can never tire,
    To my dulled vision couldst return again,
Be near, and comfort me, that I might now
    For one impassioned hour forget my pain.

The Leaf

The poplars shake their heads
Mutely in chorus.
As the rain drips from the leads,
We stare before us.

Through a cloudy mist of thought
Like thin falling rain.
And something I oft have sought
Teases my brain,

And, like each light leaf caught
From the poplars, spun
By the ruffling wind in sport,
Flutters, and is gone.

The Voice

There is a voice calling under the hill to-night.
The wind rides smooth. The stars are bright.
And I will wander for my delight
        Wherever the voice may lead me.

It is a voice that very many times I heard
When youth within me woke and stirred,
And leaped to hear the winging bird
        Though deaf to that allurement.

Not youth but hope has vanished, and to-night
Its tones are full and soft with sweet delight:
My lonely star grows misty-white,
        And I must follow the calling.

Loss

Last night as I sat
In the candle-light
Before the grate
Where the embers glowed,
I heard a traveller on the road.

Night hung clear and so still
I could plainly hear
Each step that fell
On the metalled road.
Steadily gazing, as on he strode.

Couched the moon in the sky;
And he whistled a tune
Lively and free.
Yet as he drew near
It was not unwelcome in my ear

Though forlorn and alone,
I sat there to mourn.
Strange that his tune
Woke no feeling here
In my breast! Is it thus-losing one so dear?

Vain Kisses

The tiny ripples chuckled on the beach,
    Playfully pulling at the pebbles, lapping,
Crooning, gurgling, laughing, chasing each
    In turn, and then occasionally slapping
The sides of weedy rocks just within reach.

The white cliffs reared against a burning sky,
    In hot and sullen silence staring over
That boundless bowl of undulating dye.
    We walked alone, fair nymph and youthful lover,
You, curving body slim and white, and I.

Those dreaming pools, your eyes, untroubled where
    I gazed upon still deeps in musing wonder . . .
Waved in long locks your amber-tinted hair,
    Floating on the wind that winnowed them asunder.
I kissed you then, but you were far from there.

Awake!

Wake, languorous spirit, from thy heavy sleep!
　　Already the bright glory of the day
　　Breaks forth. Flowers opening in the fields display
　　Their perfumed freshness with the first warm ray.
　　And dew-drops silver hedges 'neath the sun,
　　Beading the little toilers' wheels, all spun
　　'Ere drowsy night, soon-sped, was yet begun.
Wake, languorous spirit! Is thy sleep so deep?
　　Let not these pure delights be born again
　　For thee in vain.